Seymour Simon

INCREDIBLE SHARKS

SeaStar Books · New York

Front cover photograph: A sand tiger shark
Title page: A great white shark
Pages 2–3: A school of hammerhead sharks

This book is for my granddaughter Chloe and my grandson Jeremy.

Special thanks to reading consultant Dr. Linda B. Gambrell, Director, School of Education, Clemson University. Dr. Gambrell has served as President of the National Reading Conference and Board Member of the International Reading Association.

Permission to use the following photographs is gratefully acknowledged:
Front cover: © Jeff Rotman/Photo Researchers, Inc.; title page, pages 24–25: © C & M Fallows/Seapics.com; pages 2–3: © Eiichi Kurasawa/Photo Researchers, Inc.; pages 4–5: © Calvert Marine Museum; pages 6–7, 30–31: © David B. Fleetham/Visuals Unlimited; pages 8–9, 22–23, and back cover: © Carl Roessler; pages 10–11: © Jonathan Bird/ORG; pages 14–15: © James D. Watt/Visuals Unlimited; pages 16–17: © David Wrobel/Visuals Unlimited; pages 18–19: © Doug Perrine/ Seapics.com; pages 20–21: © Mark Jones/Minden Pictures; pages 26–27: © Richard Herrmann/Visuals Unlimited; pages 28–29: © Tom Campbell/MercuryPress.com; page 32: © Steve Drogin/Seapics.com

Library of Congress Cataloging-in-Publication Data is available.
ISBN 1-58717-238-0 (reinforced trade edition)
1 3 5 7 9 RTE 10 8 6 4 2
ISBN 1-58717-239-9 (paperback edition)
1 3 5 7 9 PB 10 8 6 4 2
PRINTED IN BELGIUM
For more information about our books, and the authors and artists who create them,
visit our web site: www.northsouth.com

The first sharks lived
more than 100 million years
before the dinosaurs.
The megalodon shark
of early times was bigger
than a school bus.

Sharks don't have any bones
in their bodies.
Their skeletons are made of
easy-to-bend cartilage.
It is just like the cartilage you
have in your nose and your ears.

Sharks can bite hard enough to make a hole in the bottom of a boat.

Some sharks have up to 3,000 razor-sharp teeth. If a shark breaks a tooth, another one takes its place.

Sharks don't chew.

They swallow each bite whole.

After a shark has a meal,

it may go for weeks

before it eats again.

A shark's skin has many sharp scales like tiny teeth. You can cut yourself by rubbing against it. These scales are magnified 1,650 times.

Sharks can hear sounds in the water half a mile away. They can smell even a single drop of blood in the water from more than a mile away.

There are about 400 kinds

of sharks.

Most of them are just

a few feet long.

The whale shark is the biggest, sometimes reaching 50 feet long. Pygmy sharks are only seven or eight inches in length. This wobbegong shark is about four feet long.

Most sharks are born live,

ready to hunt for food.

Some sharks hatch out of eggs

laid in shells or cases

on the ocean floor.

Baby sharks are called pups.

Blue sharks can give birth to

over 100 pups at one time.

Hammerhead sharks have a wide, thick head that looks like a hammer. Large hammerheads are up to 20 feet long.

The whale shark is the
biggest fish in the seas.
It can weigh as much
as three elephants.

Its six-foot mouth filters

tiny animals and plants

from the water.

The scariest shark is

the great white.

Its jaws are filled with

50 two-and-one-half-inch

sharp teeth.

Its favorite food is seals

or sea lions, not people.

Mako sharks and blue sharks
are the fastest.
They swim faster than
you can run.

Sharks will eat all sorts of strange things they find in the water.

Barrels of nails, cases of wine,
shoes, and musical instruments
have been found in the stomachs
of sharks.

Sharks do not usually
attack people.
Many more people are killed
by insect bites every year
than by sharks.
But people should not swim
in water where sharks
have been seen.

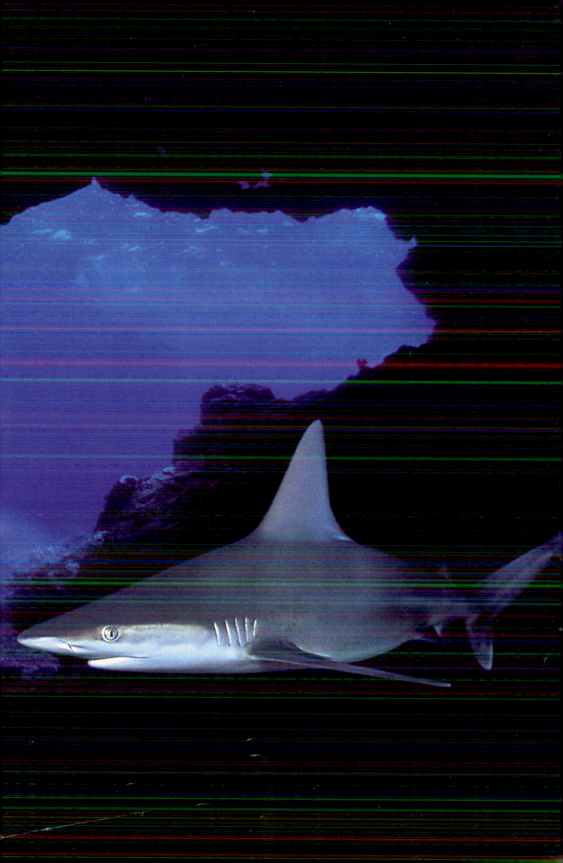

More than 30 different kinds of sharks are found each year. New facts about sharks are being discovered all the time.